ARCHANGEL

Raphael

HEALING & RESTORATION

A 33-DAY GUIDEBOOK

by

SUNNY DAWN JOHNSTON

*This guidebook is dedicated to
Archangel Raphael,
in appreciation of all of your support.*

Contents

Meet Archangel Raphael

Archangel Raphael means "God heals or God has healed"
Archangel Raphael is the angel of healing.
Helps with: Eliminating or reducing addictions and cravings, healing on all levels, guidance and support for healers, physical and spiritual eyesight, clairvoyance, and finding lost pets.
Color Vibration: Green
Gemstone: Jade or Aventurine

Invocation: I ask Archangel Raphael to surround me in his healing vibration of emerald green light. I am in need of healing at this time and I ask that you infuse me with your healing energy. Please surround me and fill me with health, well-being and wholeness. Help me to heal any wounds - physically, mentally, emotionally and spiritually - from the past or present. Heal and restore every aspect of my being for the highest good of all ... and so it is!

Journal

You can print out this guidebook and use the included journal pages or use the prompts to write in your own journal. How do you feel after reading the invocation for Archangel Raphael?

Affirmation

I am open to my healing Angels.

Journal

AFFIRMATION

I am open to my
healing Angels

DAY 2

Feel Your Heartbeat-Healing Energy

To experience Archangel Raphael's healing energy, we begin by putting your hands on your heart. As you allow your breath to move naturally through your body, just become an observer of your breath. Don't try to make it anything different than it is. After observing your breath for a few minutes, I'd like you to then visualize as you breathe. When you breathe in, you breathe in the loving energy of Archangel Raphael. See, hear, feel and know that the beautiful emerald green energy you are breathing in is healing you - mind, body and soul. See it enter in through your nose and feel the healing energy move through your entire body. Now on the exhale, hear the breath as it is released from your body and know that you have begun to allow the healing to occur. Another way to experience Raphael's energy is to focus on your breath, and as you breathe in, you breathe in love, life, healing, joy, energy, passion, etc. And as you breathe out, you release and let go of pain, sadness, frustration, anger, fear, guilt, etc. After 15 minutes, I'd like you to journal about any awareness you may have received during this experience. Just jot down anything that you became aware of. I suggest you do this exercise every night, before you go to bed, for 3 straight weeks to really connect with Archangel Raphael's energy of healing.

Journal

How could invoking Archangel Raphael every morning shift your awareness?

Affirmation

I see myself healthy and whole.

AFFIRMATION

I see myself healthy and whole

Journal

DAY 3

Cultivate the Connection

Now that you're starting your day by invoking Archangel Raphael and his protection, it's a great time to develop other rituals or routines. You can wear jewelry that contains green crystals or wear a green scarf. Find fun ways to grow your relationship with Archangel Raphael. If you have a sacred altar, you could add items that connect you to him. It could be as simple as placing a feather on your desk or hanging a green crystal from your rear-view mirror. Cultivate your relationship and you'll feel a shift in your awareness.

Journal

Why is cultivating a relationship with Archangel Raphael important to you?

Affirmation

I am open to releasing unhealthy thoughts.

Journal

AFFIRMATION

I am open to
releasing unhealthy
thoughts

6

DAY 4

Personal Experience

The loving, healing energy of Archangel Raphael saved my life. Yes, I said, saved my life. Raphael stood beside me as my most challenging physical healing occurred more than twenty years ago. This physical healing began with my pregnancy at the age of eighteen.

I had not planned to have a baby, not ever. Thoughts of an abortion crossed my mind, and I was even encouraged to have one; but when faced with the decision, I could not do it. At some deep level, I knew I was meant to have the baby, even though on the surface, I felt it was not right.

So, at age eighteen, I found myself pregnant and in a relationship with someone who drank daily, and, as you might expect, this posed many challenges. The energy that was present in our relationship was also fueled by lack: lack of money, lack of self-esteem, and lack of self-worth. This kind of energy is very heavy, and because I was not protecting my own energy, I suffered. On an energetic level, I was getting weaker and weaker, and the heaviness began to take a toll on me physically, mentally, and emotionally.

During the fourth month of my pregnancy, I developed severe toxemia, which eventually led to eclampsia: pregnancy-induced high blood pressure. The doctors prescribed strong medication for the high blood pressure and recommended complete bed rest for the remainder of my pregnancy. And when I say complete bed rest, I mean complete bed rest. The only time

I could get out of bed was to use the restroom or to go to my doctor's appointments, which were every other day. My child and I were at severe risk for seizures and liver and kidney damage, and the doctors felt bed rest would help minimize those complications. Bed rest did not sit very well with me; I am an Aries and like to go, go, go. However, something inside me knew. I could hear this whisper of a voice within me, offering to help, but I refused to allow it.

I didn't believe I deserved help. I'd made a big mistake, and this was my punishment. All my critical thinking could say was, "Sunny, you have been a very bad girl, and because of it, you now have six months to lie in this bed and think about it. You have all morning, afternoon, and evening to think about what you might have done differently."

I felt guilty, ashamed, embarrassed, humiliated, stupid, and many other negative vibrations. It was these feelings that created the toxicity in my mind that eventually manifested in my body. Today, I am very aware of how my thoughts create, but back then, all I could recognize was that I felt scared.

For the next six months, these toxic feelings continued. I alternated between feelings of depression, rage, frustration, and boredom. I cried during the times in which I had the courage to acknowledge my situation. Thoughts of "How did I end up here?" and "Why me?" frequently attacked my mind. My thoughts were just as toxic as my body, and I continued to exist in this environment for an additional two weeks past my due date. Finally, the doctors induced labor and during my twenty-sixth hour of labor, I had a mild stroke. Time was of the essence, so the doctors performed an emergency C-section; several minutes later, my son was born. I was not able to see him take his first breath since I was unconscious, but the minute I awoke, I felt pure joy as the nurse placed this beautiful baby boy in my arms. We had both made it through the hard part— at least that is what I thought.

Three days after my son's birth, I developed a low-grade fever. I was feeling out-of-sorts and not recovering the way I should. Within hours, the low-grade fever turned into a high-grade fever of 106. I broke out in hives all over my upper body, and the doctors discovered that I was oozing puss from my incision. They were uncertain of the source of the infection, so they decided to go back in surgically to see if a sponge or instrument had been left inside; however they found nothing. They had no explanation for the infection that ran rampant in my body. I was in severe physical pain, as well as emotional pain. I had seen my son for only a brief amount of time, and he was now at home and being cared for by my parents. I could not see him again because the doctors feared that I was contagious. I felt very alone . . . yet I still did not listen to that whisper of a voice within. I knew I could ask my Angels for help and healing and, because of past experiences, I did believe they could help me. But I did not feel deserving, and that lack of worthiness kept me from asking. So I continued on in pain and in resistance of the spiritual guidance that was inside me.

Much of the time that I was in the hospital, I was detached from my physical body. It was such a painful place to be, that the only way I found relief was to check out. I remember floating above my body and watching the nurses scrub the infection that had taken over my lower torso and upper thighs. Not many friends or family came to visit. I was very lonely and afraid, and I didn't want to die. How could I get through this all by myself?

The doctors continued to search for answers to the mysterious infection. They pumped me full of double and triple doses of antibiotics and performed an additional surgery to see if the source could be viewed from inside. Nothing! The 106-degree fever persisted, and I was getting weaker and weaker. The doctors finally admitted that they could do nothing to help me and asked me to sign away the rights to my son. They did not know how much longer I would live. Upon hearing those words, I felt stunned and shocked. My mind began racing. All I did was have a baby. I was young and healthy, and all I did was have baby. How could my life be ending? I couldn't believe it. I refused to believe it.

Now it was time, and I began to ask for help as I turned to that whisper of a voice within. On the eve of Mother's Day, I heard that voice within say, "I am Archangel Raphael, and I want you to call everyone you know and ask them to pray for you. Ask them to pray in whatever form of religion or belief system they have." So, I called everyone I knew and asked them to pray for me. I had decided that I wanted to live, and I wanted to see my child again. I spent many hours on the telephone, asking and trusting that each person I talked with would be there for me, supporting and holding the vision of wholeness. Twelve hours later (and three hundred-plus dollars in long-distance phone charges) my fever broke, and for the first time in two and a half weeks, I had hope.

It was a miracle. The doctors could not explain the hows and the whys, but I knew. I knew it was the support and prayers of my friends and my family, but most importantly that voice within, Archangel Raphael. For when I asked, invoked, and allowed the healing energy of Raphael, healing took place. I was open and receptive, and that is what saved my life. That evening I had made a deal with the universe. I promised to open and willing if I could just see a sign that I would be okay, that I would really make it through it all. It was the next morning that my fever broke. That was the only sign I needed.

Against doctors' orders—on the day after Mother's Day—I

checked myself out of the hospital. I had found another way to heal, and I began trusting in the healing powers of Archangel Raphael. I was a medical miracle, and I continued to work with Archangel Raphael's energy from that day forward. It took me several months to regain my strength and complete health and wholeness. Each day, I visualized an emerald-green energy around me and within me. I continued to ask Archangel Raphael for healing on an emotional and physical level. I asked for healing around the core issue of this illness. Archangel Raphael helped me to see that I had manifested this illness because I was judgmental of myself. I felt unworthy of the unconditional love and acceptance that I needed to feel from within. The only one who can love me as Spirit loves me, is me. And with that knowledge, I began to heal from the inside out. I continued to listen to that whisper and to this day, I am amazed at what messages lie within.

This experience taught me how incredibly powerful Archangel Raphael's healing energy is. Since that time, Raphael has been by my side and continues to support my students and me. Together we are teaching, those who are open, how to find the healing power within and how to work with the powerful energy of Archangel Raphael.

Journal

Have you had a personal experience like this? What did you learn from it? Are you still practicing what you learned?

Affirmation

I AM an awesome healer.

AFFIRMATION

I AM
an awesome
healer

Journal

DAY 5

Value of the Experience

When you invoke Archangel Raphael's healing energy and ask for healing with an open heart and mind, you'll receive it. When you allow the healing by opening your heart, you are healed.

Journal

What is one experience you've had recently where opening your heart could or did provide healing? How can you find the value in this experience?

Affirmation

I came to this earth equipped to be healthy and live in health.

Journal

AFFIRMATION

I came to this earth
equipped to be
healthy and live
in health

Connecting with the Angels

There is a simple four-step process that will assist you in connecting with the Archangels. Over the next four days, we'll go over this process.

Step 1: ASK
Begin by asking for assistance. For the angels to help in any area of your life, you must first "ask" for their assistance. There is no right or wrong way to do this. A simple intention works just as well as a verbal expression or a telepathic conversation. Simply saying, "Angels, please help me," is enough. Asking in a way that feels appropriate to you will ensure that the Angels will answer your call and stand by your side. The important step is to recognize that you are in need of support, guidance, direction, encouragement, etc., and be willing to ask for it.

Journal

What would it feel like to ask the Angels for help? How can you reach out and connect with Archangel Raphael?

Affirmation

My body is important to me and I am committed to taking care of it.

AFFIRMATION

My body is important
to me and
I am committed to
taking care of it

Journal

Connecting with the Angels

Step 2: ALLOW
Release the need to control the situation and be open to receive.
Allowing is as easy as "getting out of your own way." When you
release the need to control situations, people, and emotions
and just allow the flow and the laws of the Universe to work on
your behalf, then you open up room for all of the good to come
into your life. Allowing frees up your energy to do the things
that make you happy to receive the abundance that is innately
yours. Your Angels always see your life from the perspective of
allowing. They support that vision "for you" and "within you"
until you are able to feel it for yourself. The sooner you learn
to let go of resistance and start affirming what you desire, the
sooner you will come into alignment with what you are asking
for. Once the asking and allowing are in alignment with one
another, then you are well on your way to believing.

Journal

In what way have you been getting in your own way and
preventing healing? How can invoking Archangel Raphael help
you to open more?

Affirmation

*I release the pain that no longer serves the highest good and I am
open to healing.*

Journal

DAY 8

Connecting with the Angels

Step 3: BELIEVE

Trust that the Angels will guide you in perfect divine time. Trust can be one of the most difficult attitudes to adopt, especially when you do not have any evidence that you will receive what you desire. Trusting typically requires you to be vulnerable with others and, in this case, with the Angels. I made a decision a long time ago when I started working with the angelic realm, and that decision was to give up "suspicions." I made a conscious choice to be optimistic rather than pessimistic, and that choice proved to be instrumental in my working relationship with my Archangels. So it is your choice to trust that you are being guided in the perfect divine time. If you are feeling a desire from your heart, trust that that Angels will guide you in the perfect way for your highest good.

Journal

In what areas of your life can you shift a pessimistic belief into an optimistic one? You always have a choice.

Affirmation

I expand my awareness of the hidden potential in each experience.

AFFIRMATION

I expand my
awareness of the
hidden potential in
each experience

Journal

Connecting with the Angels

Step 4: RECEIVE

Listen to your intuitive guidance and give thanks. You've asked, allowed, and believed. The last step is to now receive. Your Archangels and guides will send you many messages. It could be a song on the radio, the flicker of a light, a sign on a bus or the letters on a license plate. Messages come in many ways and many forms, and I ask that you be open to receiving them in ways that may be new or different to you. As the messages and signs appear, you will find that they will validate that you are on the right path. And, finally, remember to give thanks for the abundance, joy, happiness and love that are presently in your life. Don't give up five minutes before the miracle happens. Stay open to receive all that is yours.

Journal

Are you open and ready to receive healing? Stay open to receiving signs today and journal your experience.

Affirmation

I release my body to receive healing and health.

Journal

AFFIRMATION

I release my body
to receive healing
and health

DAY 10

Time for Review

On day 2, you were given an exercise to experience Archangel Raphael's healing energy with a suggestion to try it before bed each night for 3 weeks.

Journal

How is the first week going for you? Have you noticed any changes?

Affirmation

I am allowing my body to heal itself.

AFFIRMATION

I am allowing
my body to
heal itself

Journal

DAY 11

Invocation

I now invoke the green light of Archangel Raphael to stand behind me. I ask that he pour healing over me and my relationships, past and present. I am open and grateful to receive his guidance now.

(Feel the emerald-green light in front of you and see yourself step into this light.)

Journal

Healing begins within. As you start working with Archangel Raphael on your own personal healing, you'll have opportunities to heal relationships from the past and present. How could invoking Archangel Raphael help you as you move through healing relationships?

Affirmation

I accept Archangel Raphael's healing over my relationships.

Journal

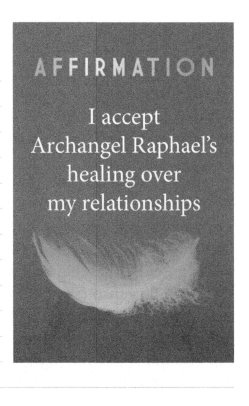

DAY 12

Release with Archangel Raphael

Sometime the healing journey can seem overwhelming. You heal one experience, and then it pops back up a few years later, or there was another layer to it that you weren't even aware of. The good news is that everything happens in Divine timing. The layers unfold just as they're meant to. You're expanding! You can choose to flow through your expansion, or kick and scream the whole way. What activities will you choose to help you remain in gratitude when expanding through a healing experience? For example, you could try journaling, a burning ceremony, an Epsom salt bath, etc.

Journal

Calling on Archangel Raphael as I feel tension rising, makes me feel . . .

Affirmation

All healing occurs in Divine timing.

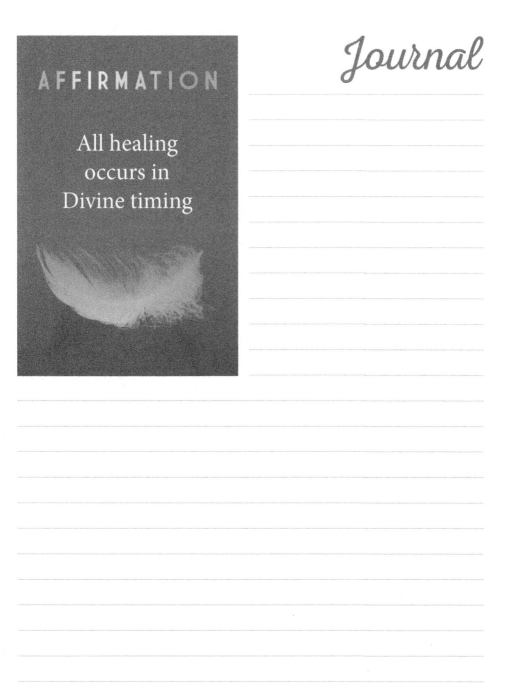

AFFIRMATION

All healing
occurs in
Divine timing

Journal

DAY 13

Moment of Reflection

There are Angels, but they don't guard you,
because they understand that well-being abounds
—Abraham-Hicks

Journal

How do you connect with your Guardian Angels throughout the day? What signs do you see? Do you ask for their guidance?

Affirmation

I call upon Archangel Raphael to increase my spiritual eyesight.

Journal

DAY 14

Invocation

Archangel Raphael, please come to me now and help me to connect to others in need of healing, with compassion. I am ready to serve as a healing force in this world.

Journal

As you develop your relationship with Archangel Raphael, how can you increase your new awareness to serve at an even greater level?

Affirmation

I know that Archangel Raphael loves me and is guiding me right now.

AFFIRMATION

I know that
Archangel Raphael
loves me and is
guiding me right now

Journal

DAY 15

Trust Yourself

Healing and growing from experiences sometimes requires us to let go of relationships or our expectations of them. Archangel Raphael can help you as you release any unhealthy relationships that no longer serve the highest good. Trust in your inner knowing, invoke Archangel Raphael to help support you and then let it go.

Journal

Are you holding onto relationships out of fear? In what ways can letting go of unhealthy relationships free you?

Affirmation

I create and surround myself with healthy relationships.

Journal

AFFIRMATION

I create and
surround myself
with healthy
relationships

D A Y 16

Creating Sacred Space

Holding onto material things and creating clutter can be an unhealthy way to protect ourselves. It's one thing to hold onto cherished items that evoke positive memories, but some things hold us stuck in the past. It could even be boxes of things you keep, just in case you need them someday. Walk through your home and identify any items that you can clear or that don't bring you joy. If it feels overwhelming, just start with 15 minutes a day or whatever feels right for you.

Journal

How can clearing the clutter help you on your healing journey? What clutter needs to go ASAP?

Affirmation

Being healthy is fun.

AFFIRMATION

Being
healthy
is fun

Journal

DAY 17

Morning Routine

On Day 2, you learned a bedtime exercise to invoke Archangel Raphael. You can also start your day with him. You can choose to create your day or your day can create you. Start by setting an intention for how you'd like to work with Archangel Raphael throughout the day. Ask for signs, people, or experiences that align with your healing journey.

Journal

My new morning routine looks like this . . .

Affirmation

I am attracting people and information that will help me live a healthy life.

Journal

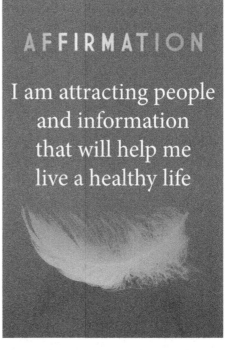

AFFIRMATION

I am attracting people
and information
that will help me
live a healthy life

DAY 18

Signs, Signs...

We see signs from the Angels every day. Sometimes they come in the form of numbers, an image, or even finding Angel feathers in what seems to be random places.

Journal

When you see signs from Archangel Raphael, how do you react? Do you dismiss them? Do you give thanks? Do you write about them?

Affirmation

I listen to and trust my intuition.

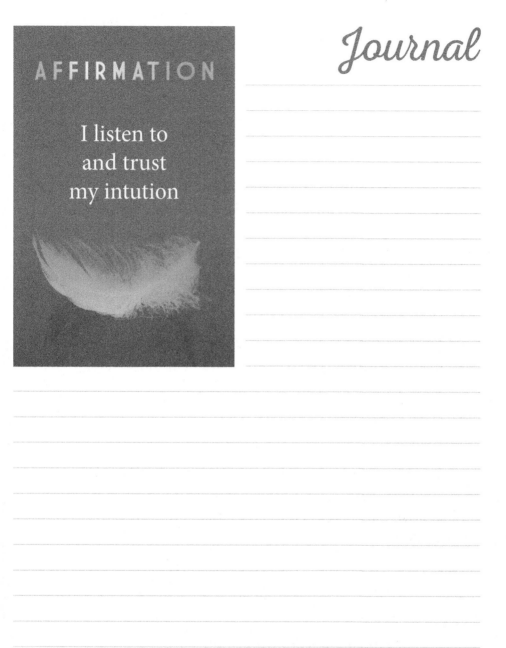

AFFIRMATION

I listen to
and trust
my intution

Journal

D A Y 19

Body Love

When we don't address healing and listen to the signs, our body can manifest illness and disease. This DIS-ease is a physical sign that we are out-of-alignment; but we are always whole, so we can choose the path toward healing at any time we want. Our physical being can manifest sickness, hold onto extra weight or many other ailments.

'*The Secret Language of your Body*' by Inna Segal is a great resource for restoring your body to it's healthiest state.

Journal

How might you have manifested illness in your life? How can working with Archangel Raphael help you to heal these areas and remove blockages? Do you see the emotional connection to your illness?

Affirmation

I release my body to accept healing and health.

Journal

AFFIRMATION

I release my body
to accept
healing and health

DAY 20

More Body Love

This body is your vehicle, as you are Spirit, embodied. If your car got a ding in the door, would you deem it worthless and ugly? Would you put fuel into it while telling it that it didn't deserve good fuel, or feel guilty about fueling it? Heck no!

Your body is yours to treat, fuel and utilize however you choose. Love your body. Release those thoughts of not being the right size or color or shape. Let it go. If you wish to create a healthier shape, go for it…from a space of loving yourself. Accept your beautiful vehicle, for it allows you to BE. Those lovely arms allow you to hug those you care about, that heart beats and keeps your blood flowing, your brain helps you form words and communicate on a physical level. The list goes on and on.

Journal

What about your body are you grateful for?

Affirmation

I am a valuable human being.

AFFIRMATION

I am a
valuable
human being

Journal

DAY 21

Invocation

I now invoke the green healing light of Archangel Raphael to assist me as I forgive myself and release anything that no longer serves my highest good. I let go with grace and ease. And so it is!

Journal

How has your awareness around healing shifted for you in the last three weeks? Have you observed yourself navigating the healing process in a different way? How present is Raphael in your life now?

Affirmation

I release my being to find its perfect healthy lifestyle, whatever that may be.

Journal

AFFIRMATION

I release my being
to find its perfect
healthy lifestyle,
whatever that may be

DAY 22

Moment of Reflection

Your cells are as depressed as you are,
and your cells are as happy and frisky as you are.
— Abraham-Hicks

Journal

How are your cells today? How can you cultivate happy and frisky cells each day?

Affirmation

My health is a priority.

AFFIRMATION

My health
is a
priority

Journal

DAY 23

Moment of Reflection

While we may be born at different places on the vibrational scale, we all possess the ability to reach the highest level through appreciation, forgiveness, joy, mediation, and love. If you wish to connect to higher vibrational beings, then you simply raise your own personal vibration.

You might be wondering why you need to raise your vibration. The universal Law of Attraction states that like energy attracts like energy; and because the beings in the spiritual realm will not lower their vibration, you must raise yours to connect with them. The more you stay in a higher, lighter, clearer vibration, the more you will connect with the spiritual realm.

Journal

Why is healing important to your spiritual journey? How important is it to you to do things that raise your vibration each day? What can you do TODAY to raise your vibration?

Affirmation

I find joy in my life each day.

Journal

AFFIRMATION

I find joy
in my life
each day

50

9 - Step Process

These next few days provide an opportunity for you to use my 9-step process on any issue or challenge, past or present, that you are not feeling in appreciation of. Take some deep breaths, focus on your heart space, invite the Archangels to surround you, and then focus on a particular issue or challenge that you want to release, forgive, heal, see a new perspective of and find appreciation for. By using these steps you can walk yourself from awareness to appreciation. If it is a current experience, you might find that you can't move immediately from where you are at this time, which is ok. Walk through the steps you have already experienced, look forward to the steps that lay ahead, invoke the Archangels, and you will begin to move, from this moment forward, toward appreciation.

So let's begin today by choosing an issue or a challenge - either past or present - and we will move through all of the steps. Once you have found appreciation in this first experience, you will have the tools to apply this shift to any other experience as well. If this is a past experience, walk yourself through each step, from where you stand today, and allow it to change your perspective of the "issue" and move you to a place of appreciation - which is also a place of forgiveness. For a current challenge, just begin with Step One. There is no right or wrong amount of time. Just take the first step, and have the willingness to move forward at whatever pace you can.

As you work through the 9-Steps, I not only ask you to think about and feel each step and your experience as you move through them, but also, to write down your experiences, one-by-one. I believe you will see and feel the power of the written word. When you write your story, the emotions begin to come up differently than in telling it.

When you see your story on paper, it brings up those emotions that can then be released. The emotions these exercises can bring up and out are profound, especially if you are feeling resistance to it. Resistance tells me the power of it is undeniable … as is the love that you have around you, the Archangels surrounding you, and the healing you have within you! Enjoy the journey!

STEP 1 - Awareness
Awareness is the state or ability to perceive, to feel, or to be conscious of. Typically you become aware of a challenge, an illness, an emotion, or a desire. You can also have self-awareness. Self-awareness is the ability to perceive one's own existence, traits, feelings and behaviors. You become aware of your own personality or individuality.

Journal

What issue or challenge are you ready to release through this healing process? What will it feel like to have released this issue?

Affirmation

I release my body to find its perfect weight, whatever that may be.

AFFIRMATION

I release my body
to find its perfect
weight, whatever
that may be

Journal

DAY 25

9 - Step Process

STEP 2 - Look Within

You have to have a willingness to look within and ask for help. Unfortunately, many of us look outside of ourselves for answers to our questions. The key is to get in touch with the inner you, and acknowledge the intuitive power that you have. Oftentimes decisions are based from the ego and not the spirit. By looking within, the path becomes clear and uncluttered.

Journal

What experience have you had with this lately? Where have you been focusing on someone or something outside of yourself? How can you shift your awareness by going within?

Affirmation

I have the power to heal my mind, body and spirit.

Journal

AFFIRMATION

I have the power
to heal my
mind, body
and spirit

9 - Step Process

STEP 3 - Choice

Choice simply means the act of choosing. You always have a choice to act or react. The kind of life you have is the life you choose. In this process, choice is the foundation of change. Sometimes you perceive your choice as a right choice or a wrong choice; but my point is – you still have a choice.

Journal

What areas of your life do you need to make a choice in? Why haven't you? Remember, not choosing is still a choice.

Affirmation

Archangel Raphael's healing light surrounds me as I see myself as whole and loved.

AFFIRMATION

Archangel Raphael's healing light surounds me as I see myself as whole and loved.

DAY 27

9 - Step Process

STEP 4 - Commitment
The most important single factor in an individual's healing success is commitment. Commitment ignites action. To commit means to devote yourself to a purpose or cause.

Journal

What commitment are you willing to make to yourself and your own personal healing? In this commitment, are you overextending yourself and setting yourself up for sabotage or not really making a major step? Remember, you, your health and relationships suffer when you don't maintain your commitments.

Affirmation

I am committed to my health and well-being.

Journal

AFFIRMATION

I am committed
to my health
and well-being

DAY 28

9 - Step Process

STEP 5 - Responsibility

Responsibility means accepting that you and you alone are accountable for your life. There is no one to blame. Being responsible comes with the realization that you are where you are because of your own conduct, beliefs, and behavior. Your choices have created the experiences you are living right now. The good news is that you are responsible for your life. The bad news is that you are responsible for your life.

Journal

What responsibility are you carrying that is not yours? Is it time to give it up and let it go? Conversely, what responsibility do you need to acknowledge? How can you accomplish either one of these today? What is one step you can take today in regards to responsiblity?

Affirmation

Now that I know better, I do better.

AFFIRMATION

Now that I
know better,
I do better

DAY 29

9 - Step Process

STEP 6 - Action

Action is the state or process of acting or doing something in order to achieve a purpose. In this step, you take action and you invoke the healing energy of the Archangels.

Journal

What is one action step you can take today towards your awareness? It only need to be a step; and each day, as you take action you begin to heal.

Affirmation

I take action to create a healthy and abundant life.

Journal

9 - Step Process

STEP 7 - Releasing and Replenishing

Releasing is often defined as an emotional purging.
Our emotions, thoughts, and beliefs are contained in our bodies
… so learning to release these will help you achieve more peace,
happiness and emotional well-being. Replenishing simply means
to fill back up or make complete again. Emotional purging often
leaves empty spaces within - and since nature abhors a vacuum,
you must fill yourself back up.

Journal

You have to let it go and then fill it back up, almost immediately.
What are you willing to let go of today and how are you going
to replenish it? What exactly will you do in order to release and
then replace the energy? Both steps are critical in healing body,
mind and soul. Remember, you have to replace it.

Affirmation

*I release any attachments to old stories, self-sabotage and
unhealthy habits.*

AFFIRMATION

I release any attachments to old stories, self-sabotage and unhealthy habits

Journal

9 - Step Process

STEP 8 - Maintenance

In this case, maintenance means continually showing up for your healing and restoration. It is important to be open to the healing. If you don't do this, you risk staying stuck and repeating unhealthy experiences - physical, emotional, mental and spiritual.

Journal

In order to maintain my health and well-being, I need to _____.
When I feel off, I will _____ to support me in maintaining my own energy.

Affirmation

I learn from my life experiences with grace and ease.

Journal

9 - Step Process

STEP 9 - Appreciation
Appreciation is knowing or understanding the value of an experience and is often expressed with feelings of gratitude. In this step, it specifically means to honor an experience with open arms and a healed heart. Oftentimes, once appreciation is experienced, forgiveness follows.

Journal

When I look back a week ago, I see that the initial challenge I had has served me by? I can now see that the value in my experience was _____.

Affirmation

I appreciate my healing journey.

AFFIRMATION

I appreciate my
healing journey

DAY 33

The Journey Continues

Although, this is the end of this guidebook, your journey with Archangel Raphael will continue to grow. Commit to your new daily practices and continue to cultivate the relationship you have developed with him.

Journal

Why is continuing a relationship with Archangel Raphael important to you? What are at least five ways that you can maintain this relationship?

Affirmation

I AM LOVE - I AM LIGHT - It is great to be me!

Journal

AFFIRMATION

I AM LOVE
I AM LIGHT
It is great to be me!

If you enjoyed the Archangel Raphael
Mandala Coloring Sheet on the previous page,
please visit our interactive website:
www.sunnydawnjohnston.com/mandalas
for more detailed information about
the Symbols and Archangels.

Share your completed artwork, see what
others have created and connect with like
minds too.

Other Books by Sunny Dawn Johnston

Archangel Michael: Maintain Your Energy
Invoking the Archangels
Invoking the Archangels Workbook
Living Your Life Purpose with Sunny Dawn Johnston
& Friends
Find Me
No Mistakes
The Love Never Ends
Answers About the Afterlife
The Wedding Officiant's Manual
365 Days of Angel Prayers
Healing Mandalas Coloring Book
Doodles & Dalas Coloring Book

Available Here:
http://sunnydawnjohnstonboutique.com/product-category/
books/

Also available on Amazon.com
and other online retailers.

Made in the USA
Las Vegas, NV
06 December 2023

82090872R10046